The Natural Rearing

H B Turner

To all the fur-kids I have ever and will ever have the privilege of assisting or simply attending your whelp, you will always have a place in my heart.

About the Author

In 1999, on return from a business trip to America, H B Turner (Hope) bought a raw fed kitten. Other than the bones she remembered getting from the butcher for her beloved Chow Chow as a child, this was her first introduction to raw feeding.

In 2002, Hope found a dog she fell in love with and started researching further, as the dog was raw fed. In early 2003, she then bought two raw fed puppies and the research began in earnest, including taking a number of short courses on behaviour, nutrition, natural health and communication and her first litter was born in 2004.

Having believed that she had exhausted the non-academic route of learning, in 2009 Hope returned to full time education, taking first a Foundation Degree in Animal Management and Welfare, and then 'topping up' to a Bachelor's Degree in Applied Animal Studies in 2012. Throughout her studies each assignment was tailored as much as possible to scientific research on the differentials between raw and conventional feeding, natural rearing and its benefits.

During this time, Hope chose to use social media as a platform to teach what she had learnt and created a number of recipes which she believed were healthier than many of the market alternatives. She also spent a great deal of time researching details behind behaviour and natural remedies.

Hope released her first book "The Science Behind Raw Feeding" in May 2013, lectures at seminars on raw feeding, is currently taking time out from her Master's Degree to work on further books, has recently launched her own radio show and animal welfare campaign and is hoping to start a Canine Nutrition Clinic in the near future.

For details of how to get hold of her, go to her website at:

www.healthful.uk.com

Contents

Introduction

Natural Rearing Breeders aim to improve the health and temperament of each generation of animals via planned artificial selection, tempered by individual preference and bolstered by natural health. In order to be able to select these criteria, health testing and specific rearing practices are utilised. This book is aimed at showing you what practices they might follow, and to teach you to do the same should you wish to be a natural rearing breeder.

In this book you will find examples of current practices, recommendations for health testing and selection of breeding stock, natural remedies, details of what occurs during gestation and parturition as well as illustrations along the way.

If you are looking for, or seeking homes for a naturally reared pet, please join us on our Facebook group the 'Natural Breeders Register UK'.

Health regime

In order to be considered a Natural Rearing Breeder, everything given to the animals should be natural in origin and have gone through no or minimal processing. Whilst tags and collars are a legal requirement, many natural rearing breeders will not microchip, due to the risks of cancer and other problems from the process, for further details check www.chipmenot.com.

Feeding

Feeding a raw, species appropriate diet is a huge part of ensuring the health of the animal in question and that of future generations (Pottenger, 1983). A natural diet has been scientifically shown to boost not only the immune system, but also the health of each individual cell in the body (Turner, 2013) and therefore is a great foundation for health.

There are many books available on raw feeding, discussing a great number of varieties of diet, for more details on the reasons why natural rearing breeders believe that raw is best, read "The Science Behind Canine Raw Feeding" by H B Turner (shameless plug).

Environment and Exercise

A clean and healthy environment, with plenty of space to stretch and play is essential. As long as the animal is getting enough exercise at home, 'walks' need not be necessary, and should only be had, if it is a pleasurable experience for both of you. Stress is known to adversely affect the immune system and therefore can impact both your and your pets' health.

If you do struggle to have an enjoyable walk, I recommend the book "Wish Come True" by A K L Withers (available via amazon); Abbie includes a number of examples of dogs with both home and walk related behavioural issues and describes how the use of her method can reverse these problems and lead to a healthier, happier relationship with your dog.

For natural cleaning of indoor accidents, white vinegar, baking soda and lemon juice prove very useful, getting rid of stains and smells alike, without the risk that harsh chemicals can bring to sensitive paws and lungs. Steam cleaning is also a natural, chemical free way to ensure a healthy environment.

N.B. Be aware that whilst bleach is known to destroy parvo virus, and is regularly used as a cheap disinfectant, it reacts badly with ammonia, exponentially increasing odour when it comes into contact with urine.

Medical Needs

Whilst there is no doubt that science has advanced medical technology to great heights and that pharmaceuticals have their place in veterinary practice, all pharmaceuticals have side effects, which can have a knock on effect on health.

Vaccines are no exception; in fact they have been shown to have a negative impact on the immune system, not to work, have horrific side effects (including death) and even to lead the animal to contract the disease from the vaccine itself. For more information on the risks of vaccines, I recommend the books 'Shock to the System' and 'What Vets don't tell you about Vaccines' by Catherine O'Driscoll of Canine Health Concern.

Diets can be tailored to individual needs, by the additions of certain nutraceuticals, for example food stuffs with anti-biotic, anti-microbial and anti-fungal properties (e.g. honey) and/or herbal ingredients known to cause certain reactions (e.g. milk thistle for liver issues, slippery elm and live yogurt for digestive disorders etc.).

As well as food additions, there are other natural remedies available for certain health issues, i.e. homeopathy, flower remedies etc. Natural topical treatments (e.g. colloidal silver) and even natural treatments for fleas (e.g. garlic, neem) and worming (e.g. Verm-X, diatomaceous earth), as opposed to their chemical alternatives which have been known to cause epilepsy and even death.

11

Natural rearing breeders turn to natural remedies rather than chemical ones as much as possible. I recommend that any advice followed or books purchased are taken from or written by recognised experts, as the old saying 'a little knowledge is a dangerous thing', is more than applicable when it comes to health. Sadly I have witnessed many health issues exacerbated by bad advice, from people who are not thoroughly versed on the subject, and that old favourite 'I've been doing this for years' is no guarantee of correct knowledge.

If in any doubt at all, please contact your local registered veterinary surgeon with regard to any treatment you may wish to give, for details of your nearest homeopathic vet go to www.bahvs.com in the UK and www.ahvma.org in America, other countries also have holistic veterinary associations.

Many veterinary surgeons will recommend spaying and neutering, however this has an un-natural effect on hormonal homeostasis, and has been shown to increase the risk of certain cancers in both males and females, increases the likelihood of bladder problems in females and is known to reduce lifespan; therefore many natural rearing breeders keep their animals entire and require that their puppy buyers do the same.

In my natural emergency kit, I have (Table 1):

	What I use it for:-
Homeopathy	
Aconite	Shock
Arnica	Bruising
Belladonna	Heat (i.e. I have used it successfully

	for mastitis)
Bach Flower Remedies	
Rescue Remedy	Stress
Nutraceuticals	
Aloe Vera	Wound moisturiser
Coconut Oil	Wound moisturiser
Colloidal Silver	Anti-biotic (both topical and oral)
*Garlic	Immune booster
Honey	Anti-biotic, Anti-microbial, Anti-fungal (both topical and internal)
Live Yogurt	Digestive issues
Slippery Elm	Digestive issues
Spirulina	Energy boost
Thornit Canker Powder	Ear issues i.e. wax/mites

Table 1

*Garlic: Be aware that too much garlic can have a toxic effect and shut down the kidneys, this is at a level equivalent to 1 clove per kilogram of dog.

Rules/Code of Ethics

It is always advisable to follow your local Kennel Club rules and codes of ethics, as well as being up to date with local animal welfare law.

- Kennel Club Code of Ethics (Appendix 1) should be being adhered to, as will the Animal Welfare Act 2006 (Crown, 2006).
- All practices in line with the Kennel Club Accredited Breeder Scheme (Appendix 2) should be followed, other than any which enforce artificial chemicals.
- Health records to be kept for all stock and puppies.
- Copies of health tests and DNA profiles should be lodged with the relevant breed club
- All puppies should be registered with the breed club/Kennel Club
- Young from un-registered animals will not be recognised by the breed club or Kennel Club

Examples of a Hip X-ray (Image 1), Hip Score (Image 2), Eye Test (Image 3) and DNA Profile (Image 4) follow.

Example Hip X-ray

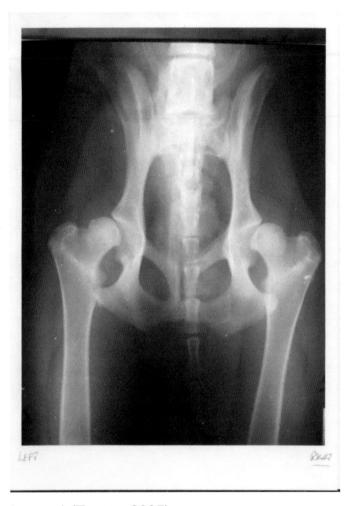

Image 1 (Turner, 2005)

Example Hip Score

BRITISH VETERINARY ASSOCIATION/KENNEL CLUB HIP DYSPLASIA SCHEME

To: British Veterinary Association
7 Mansfield Street, London W1G 9NQ
Telephone: 020 7636 6541

05 - [redacted]

THE ORIGINAL OF THIS
CERTIFICATE IS GREEN

Owner's Declaration
(PLEASE COMPLETE USING BLOCK CAPITALS AND BLACK INK)

KC Registered Number _327_

KC Registered Name ......

Breed ...... Sex _DoG_ Date of birth ......

Name of owner ...... Address ......

Sire:	PGS:
	PGD:
Dam:	MGS:
	MGD:

I hereby declare that (NB: DELETION OF ANY OF THESE ITEMS INVALIDATES THIS CERTIFICATE)
(a) The particulars above are correct and relate to the dog submitted today for radiographic examination
(b) This dog is a minimum of one year old and has not previously been scored under the scheme
(c) I give permission for a copy of the certificate to be sent to the geneticist retained by the breed society or other representative body
(d) I give permission for the results of the examination to be used at a future date for the purpose of statistical research
(e) I give permission for the result to be published and included on the relevant KC documents

Owner's signature ...... Date _10/10/05_

Submitting Veterinary Surgeon's Certificate (PLEASE COMPLETE USING BLOCK CAPITALS AND BLACK INK)

Microchip/tattoo number (if known): [redacted]

I certify that the radiograph relating to the dog
identified above was taken on the following date _10/10/05_
and in conformity with the provisions of the HD Scheme Procedure Notes

Veterinary surgeon submitting radiograph (BLOCK CAPITALS) ......

Address ......

Post code ......

Date _10-10-05_ Signed ...... MRCVS

Please submit the correct fee for the radiograph to be processed (cheques payable to BVA.) For current fees contact BVA

CERTIFICATE OF SCORING

HIP JOINT	Score Range	Right	Left	
Norberg angle	0-6	O	I	NB The scores represent the opinion of the BVA appointed scrutineers for the radiograph submitted. The lower the score, the less evidence of hip dysplasia present. Please consult the current procedure notes and breed mean score sheet for relevant details (available from BVA)
Subluxation	0-6	I	3	
Cranial acetabular edge	0-6	2	2	
Dorsal acetabular edge	0-6	—		
Cranial effective acetabular rim	0-6	—		
Acetabular fossa	0-6	—		
Caudal acetabular edge	0-5	—		
Femoral head/neck exostosis	0-6	—		
Femoral head recontouring	0-6	—		
TOTALS (max possible 53 per column)		3	6	9 Total score (max possible 106)

WE HEREBY CERTIFY that the score of the radiograph submitted for the dog identified
above was produced using the scoring criteria of the BVA/Kennel Club Hip Dysplasia Scheme

Date 0 7 NOV 2005

Signed ...... F/MRCVS Signed _LE Barnes_ F/MRCVS 1/97

Image 2 (Turner, 2005)

Example Eye test

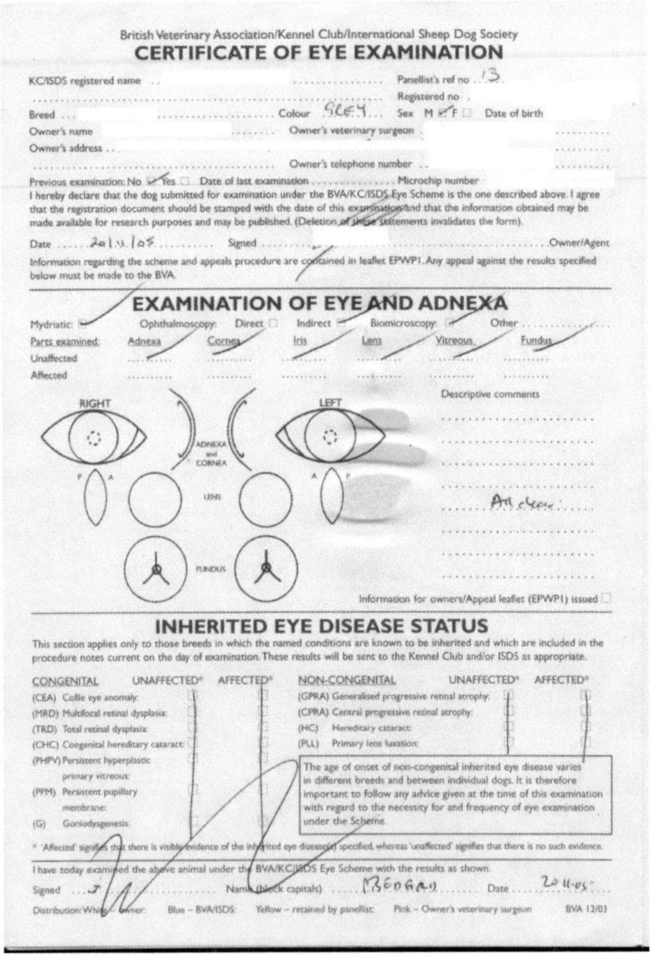

Image 3 (Turner, 2005)

Example DNA Profile

Image 4 (Turner, 2005).

Blood Lines

DNA profiling is important to establish lines (Kennel Club, 2010), as any breed is susceptible to bad policies and fraudulent pedigrees, thus perpetuating in-breeding without the responsible breeders' knowledge. If all stock is DNA tested and registered on file with the relevant breed club, then lineage can be scientifically verified.

DNA details are now listed on DNA profiles, with 23 pairs of numbers, whereas before these lists were sent separately to the profile certificate.

These numbers relate to the size of the gene at a particular locus (location) on the segment tested. As all genetic material comes from one or other of the parents, (half from each) these can be matched up to prove lineage.

For example:

Mother	– Locus 1	236/242
Father	– Locus 1	198/206
Offspring	– Locus 1	206/242

If you are sure that the lineage is correct, but these numbers do not match up, then it could either be a mutation or a mistake may have occurred in the DNA software at the laboratory.

Health Screening

Health screening via use of the BVA/KC Health Schemes (Kennel Club, 2006) is an important part of selecting breed quality animals (Carricato, 1992), and must be based on historic health issues within the breed and its' founder breeds (Gough & Thomas, 2004).

Therefore the following tests are recommended:

DNA profiling (Kennel Club, 2, 2006) of all current stock and young.

For potential breed stock (but constructive to have in all stock):

Hip Scoring via BVA/KC Hip Dysplasia Scheme

Eye Testing via BVA/KC/ISDS Eye Scheme

Specific breeds may have other health issues, i.e. von Willebrands disease (a blood clotting disorder), elbow scoring etc. therefore any testing available should be done if appropriate.

Evaluation of Temperament

Temperament is also of great importance, and should be evaluated (Carricato, 1992) in each case when considering the breeding potential of stock. A constructive way to do this, and have an official record, is with Pets as Therapy (PAT) testing (Pets As Therapy, 2010), where animals tested to be of sound temperament visit old peoples' homes/hospitals etc. (Image 5).

Image 5 (Turner, 2005)

Reproductive Technologies

Some of todays' latest technology could prove very useful and could enlarge the gene pool of any specific breed.

Cloning

The cloning of dogs was first achieved in 2005 at Seoul National University in South Korea, via the use of 1,095 embryos, being implanted into 123 females, resulting in 1 live pup (Lee *et al.* 2005). This process, now refined and commercially available, could be of tremendous use to any breed with restricted lineage, where neutered /spayed animals, or those too old to reproduce, but of diverse genetics could be rejuvenated, in order to increase the gene pool.

Initial costs were prohibitive due to the success ratio, however this process has recently been made more affordable by new techniques (BBC, 2009), and may be made more reliable by using eggs from established bitches (Loi *et al.* 2008).

It must be noted however that the cloning of an older dog, does have its limitations, as the lifespan of clones is often not as long as that of those naturally conceived (Ogonuki *et al.* 2002). With this in mind, it is suggested that these cloned dogs are very carefully bred young i.e. bitches 1st season after health checks, males soon after (hip scores and eye tests are done at twelve months of age), to naturally conceived animals, and that their offspring are also put to naturally conceived animals.

Artificial Insemination

Semen from intact males can be collected and frozen in liquid nitrogen for future use, this can be stored for years, or immediately transported and artificially inseminated into a bitch who is tested to be sufficiently in heat to promote fertilisation (Holst, 2000).

Cryogenic freezing of sperm of animals outside the country for import and artificial insemination, in line with Kennel Club requirements (Kennel Club, 3, 2006), could aid genetic diversity, and prevents the need for pet passports and transport, reducing the risk of over-vaccination.

The freezing of sperm unfortunately often reduces its' motility, reducing the likelihood of pregnancy (Carricato, 1992), with a 65-85% success rate, with probable small litters (Thomassen *et al.* 2001), however, if faced with a small gene pool, it could prove invaluable.

Choosing a Stud

Once you have established that your bitch is of breed quality, having passed all relevant health checks and been determined breed stock by the relevant dog club, it is imperative to choose your stud dog wisely (Frankling, 1987).

Obviously you will require a stud dog that has all the correct health certifications, has a great temperament and adheres to the breed standard (Image 6). He must also be not too closely related to your bitch, and you will need to know what *issues or colours may be carried in his line.

Image 6 (Turner, 2005)

If you are not completely aware of what lines carry what colours and health issues, this choice can be assisted by the Club breed adviser, who will have details on the pedigrees and genetic histories of all recommended stud dogs, and can predict not only any potential genetic issues, but even colours of potential young.

Whilst the new breeder may be keen to use the stud dog belonging to a friend or available locally, this match may not be recommended. Un-recommended matches by breed advisors have previously proven predictions of un-saleable colours and even health issues. It is of major importance that the genetics of future generations be taken into account, so careful planning with the advice of the breed club is necessary.

*Issues in this case may mean any number of things, from digestive disorders, to an unsteady temperament, epilepsy and even dwarfism

Courtship and Mating

Bitches season every six months, dependent on breed from around 6-10 months of age, although there are a few who have been known to season annually.

The time in between seasons is called anestrous, when a bitch first comes into heat, this stage is called proestrus and normally lasts around 10 days; her vulva will begin to swell, she will begin to bleed and personality traits may be altered (Holst, 2000).

Many bitches are very clean when in season, and you may not notice the bleeding, or they may not bleed at all, known as a 'silent season'. One of the easiest indicators that a bitch is coming into season, is the difference in attitude of any entire males that may be around. I tend to use the rule of thumb that once I've noticed the bleeding, it's probably about day 3.

When the bitch is 10-12 days into her season, (in oestrus) she will begin to stand for the stud, who will have been attempting to mount for a few days if un-proven. When the bitch stands she will elevate her vulva and hold her tail to one side (Holst, 2000) so that the dog can mount; whilst he will grab hold of her with his front legs, moving her pelvis closer to his own, in order to gain entry, and begin thrusting movements (Image 7).

Image 7 (Turner, 2005)

Upon full penetration they will 'tie' and turn back to back (Image 8), this occurs via the combination of swelling of the base of the males' penis and the constriction of the females vaginal sphincter (Mech, 1970), and has been seen to last between 7 and 45 minutes in some breeds of dog. The 'tie' ensures that the full three stages of ejaculate are kept within the female reproductive tract (Neville, 1993). Only the second stage contains semen, however the third stage aids transport (Holst, 2000).

Image 8 (Turner, 2005)

Should either the bitch or the dog not be interested in reproducing with your chosen mate, it is advisable not to force it. Animals can literally smell genetic incompatibilities through pheromones (Penn, 2002), if they decide they are not compatible, be ruled by Mother Nature and start the selection process again.

Gestation and Parturition

Whilst the ovulation process involves the same hormones as found in humans, i.e. hormonal production and release from the hypothalamus, stimulating hormone release from the anterior pituitary gland, initiating follicle growth and ovulation, as does the conception process, i.e. release of hormones from the corpus luteum, zygote and endometrium, and there is a 'ovulation test kit' available for dogs, there is no 'pregnancy test kit', as the hormones found in the urine do not alter due to pregnancy.

Therefore most breeders are not sure of pregnancy until there are noticeable personality differences in the bitch or pregnancy is evident through uterine enlargement. Whilst may veterinary surgeries and independent experts can offer x-rays in order to verify pregnancy and numbers, this is just as risky for dogs as it is for humans, and was banned in human medicine over 50 years ago, therefore it is not recommended. Ultra-sound technology, can also verify pregnancy and numbers, however ultra-sound has recently been linked with autism and other issues, due to the heat produced by the equipment itself (Williams & Casanova, 2011:Olson, 2009) and by the time you get to the stage in the pregnancy where an ultra-sound would show useful results, I don't believe it is worth bothering with, let the number and sexes be a pleasant surprise.

One to six weeks

During this time the bitch may show no outward signs of pregnancy, she does not need extra food and need not be restricted from exercise (Williams, 2009). By five weeks there may be a visible difference in stomach girth, but don't panic if you can't see one.

Six to nine weeks

During this time the bitches' food intake needs to increase by around 10% per week, up to 50% more than her normal diet by the due date (Evans & White, 1988).

The bitch should be wormed from the 42nd day of pregnancy to the 2nd day post whelping (Lane & Cooper, 2003), this is due to the fact that worm in the bitch can travel to and infect the pups within the womb, as well as travelling into the mammary glands, and infecting milk production. Liquid Panacur 10% (Eldredge *et al.* 2007) is a chemical treatment that has been recommended, however there are natural alternatives that have been shown to work including Verm-X (Veterinary recommended) and/or Diatomaceous Earth, the makers of Verm-X (www.verm-x.com) have a good customer service team who can advise you on correct amounts for your bitch.

By 7 weeks you may be able to see movement of a pup or two whilst Mum is on her side, look towards her groin area; I must admit I do enjoy watching them fidget, although I'm sure it isn't the most comfortable thing for Mum.

At this stage I stop off-property excursions for all resident dogs, and do not allow any visiting dogs, due to the risks of the transfer of disease from other dogs or wild animals. If possible I maintain outdoor and indoor shoes, if not I spray the soles of shoes with disinfectant when returning to the property and maintain this until the pups are at least six weeks of age.

Towards the very end of the pregnancy, fur from around the nipples will start to come away, nipples will become engorged and may start to produce milk.

The Birthing process

A "Newborn Birthing Box" (AMP, 2010) is cheap, hygienic and easy to dispose of after use. Layer thickly with newspaper topped with clean vetbed (Petlife, 2011) and/or blankets, pig rails need to be fitted once whelping is complete (Root Kustritz, 2006), to help prevent accidental laying of the mother on the puppies.

Expose the bitch to the birthing box in a quiet corner away from other dogs, from a week or two prior to her due date. Around two to three days prior to the onset of labour, the bitch will begin nesting, by ripping up the paper in the whelping box. Within 24 hours of labour her temperature will go down by one degree (Carricato, 1992), she will become restless, not be able to settle, will pace back and forth and separate herself from other dogs.

New mothers often require assistance, as this is an exhausting process which can last up to 30 hours, with time between puppies anywhere from 8 minutes to 3 hours. I often have a hot water bottle to hand for warming purposes, as well as artery clamps, in case the cord is cut too close to the pup and bleeds.

A birthing chart is advised as per the example in table 2 below:

Dam	Name	Hip score	4:3	Eye test	Clear	Age	26 months
Sire	Name	Hip score	3:3	Eye test	Clear	Age	25 months

Due date	10/03/2004				
Parturition date	09/10 March 2004				

Time	Sex	Afterbirth	Weight	Suck reflex	Any faults	Colour/ description

Table 2

In next series of images (Image 9 - 13), you can see the pup still inside its' sac (foetal membranes), with the placenta still inside the bitch, followed by the removal of the sac by the mother.

Image 9 (Robinson, 2005)

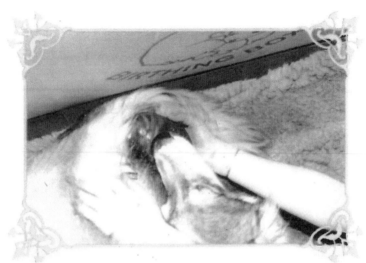

Image 10 (Robinson, 2005)

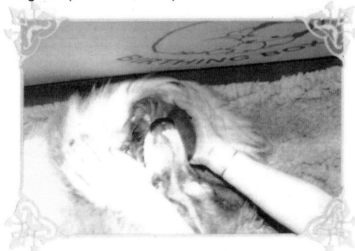

Image 11 (Robinson, 2005)

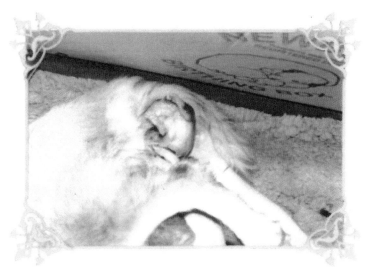

Image 12 (Robinson, 2005)

Image 13 (Robinson, 2005)

In the following images (Images 14 – 19), you can observe the handler, holding the umbilical cord close to the puppy, this helps to prevent the risk of umbilical hernias, whilst allowing the mother to cut the cord.

If the mother will not cut the cord, or you fear she is cutting too close to the pup, there is a natural tear point around an inch or two away from the belly, this can be felt with your fingers and with a little applied nail pressure can be pulled apart without the risk of bleeding.

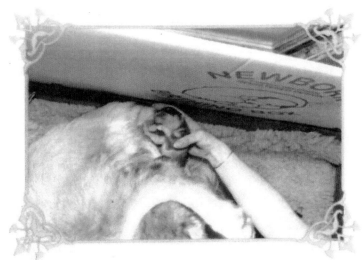

Image 14 (Robinson, 2005)

Image 15 (Robinson, 2005)

Image 16 (Robinson, 2005)

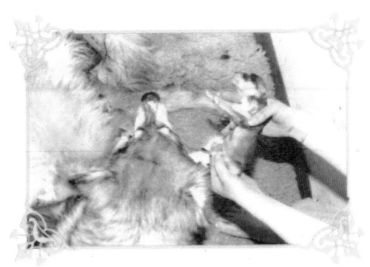

Image 17 (Robinson, 2005)

Image 18 (Robinson, 2005)

Image 19 (Robinson, 2005)

These are photographs were taken for instructional purposes, are of a typical birth with minor assistance and without complications, however, these can occur. In my experience I have on occasion had to reach inside the vagina, to assist with a pup whose head was either stuck behind the pelvis, or who had started to inch up the other horn of the uterus. This can be tricky and requires complete trust between yourself and the bitch. If you are not sure of how to handle such a situation, it is advisable to have someone with you at this time who is experience with whelping, if not, then an expensive (as Murphy's law ensures that whelping occurs out of hours) call to a veterinary surgeon may be necessary.

Once separate from mother, immediately ensure that any amniotic fluid in the mouth or nose that may be hindering breathing is removed. Dry with a warm clean towel, and once the placenta has been expelled, attach the pup to a nipple for mother and puppy to bond; this also promotes the release of oxytocin which aids with bonding and contractions for further births (Riviere & Papich, 2009). It is important to check that each pups' placenta is discharged due to the risk of pyometra, and to weigh each pup for future health checks (Holst, 2000).

Checking the suck reflex is essential, do this by gently inserting the tip of a clean finger into the mouth, if the puppy sucks, great, if it does not, it may be weak, already fading, or have a cleft palette. Weak pups can sometimes be revived through warming and ensuring that they attain colostrum (the first milk feed from Mum). Pups with a cleft palette require hand feeding and often fail to thrive, if they are not indeed still born.

Most breeds are good self whelpers, with few issues of dystocia being reported, but check the history on your own breed. Puppies should be strong, but don't be too surprised by fading puppy syndrome, it happens in all breeds, for a wide variety of reasons. The pup may seem ok to start with, but fails to feed, and life appears to fade away from it.

On occasion a particularly large litter may require extra feeding to assist the bitch (Image 20), there are several commercial milk substitutes i.e. Welpi (Petlife, 2, 2011), however fresh raw goats milk is highly recommended, as it has a fat content much closer to that of dogs milk, than anything derived from cows' milk.

Image 20 (Turner, 2008)

Care and Management of young

One to three weeks

For the first three weeks the mother will care for the pups, feeding (Image 21) and cleaning them virtually constantly (McLeavy, 1996). Keep other animals away (Fennell, 2005) and clean out the whelping box regularly i.e. around 6-8 times a day. The bitch will be reticent to stray far from the pups (Fennell, 2005) to begin with, but will need to for toileting, feeding etc.

As young pups cannot regulate their own temperature (Fennell, 2005), ensure that the whelping box is kept warm, a heat lamp is useful here, however only allow the heat to cover half of the box, so that the pups and Mum can move away if necessary, preventing over heating; it is also a good idea to have a window open near the pups for fresh ventilation (Holst, 2000).

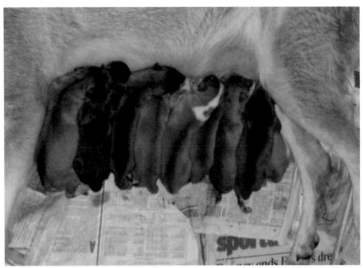
Image 21 (Turner, 2005)

Hind dew claws that have no bone can be removed by a vet or experienced breeder at 3-4 days of age (Holst, 2000), and other claws will require regular clipping after two weeks of age, to help to reduce scratching of the mothers teats (Evans & White, 1988). It is important to keep up throughout the life of any dog, as overgrown nails can impact the standing position and therefore the strength of muscles in the lower legs. It is illegal to dock tails, and doing so would not be in keeping with natural rearing anyway. Puppies should also be wormed at two weeks of age (Holst, 2000) and every fortnight thereafter until 8 weeks, then once at 12 weeks and every three months until 1 year old. Natural means of worming, have already been detailed.

Table 2 (page 38) can be referred and added to, it is also advisable to keep weight records of each pup, daily up to 10 days and then weekly to be sure of healthy growth (Holst, 2000: Evans & White, 1988). The pups weight should double in the first week to 10 days, after which I cease to worry about weight gain, as the majority of risk is over. Check for 'baggyness', the pups should be plump at all times, if they feel 'baggy', there may be a problem.

The mother will need to be on increased food at a rate of three to four times her normal daily allowance by the third to fourth week (size of litter dependent) (Evans & White, 1988) and have access to plenty of fresh water.

At around 10 days the pups eyes will open and they will start to socialise properly (Mason, 1973), at this time their ear canals start to open and they begin to hear (Fennell, 2005).

Nothing can quite prepare you for both the joy and the exhaustion associated with having a litter of puppies in the house. For the first 3 weeks be prepared to not get much, if any, sleep. I tend to have the whelping box next to my bed, so that should any puppies get stuck under mum (pig-rails not withstanding), I can simply lean over, pull them out and 'plug them in' (Image 22), i.e. latch them on to a nipple so that they immediately get a burst of oxytocin, increasing their bond with Mum, and relieving their stress from being stuck underneath her.

Image 22 (Turner, 2013)

Three weeks to eight weeks

Three to four weeks is the natural age for pups to want to start to explore and for the mother to introduce them to the rest of the pack (Mason, 1973). Therefore the whelping box, with a surrounding puppy pen, preferably with fold-down door enabling mother to come and go at will, can be moved into the main living area, this also simulates what would naturally happen in the wild with the dam moving the pups at about this time for protection (Mason, 1973) and will not alarm the mother. At this time a shallow bowl of water can be added for the puppies to lap at (Fennell, 2005).

Here the same litter as in Image 21 pictured at around four weeks old, puppies need lots of sleep (Fennell, 2005) (Image 23):

Image 23 (Turner, 2005)

This is also when pups need to start being fed solid food, starting out with soft food (Image 24) three to four times a day (Holst, 2000) and graduating to harder food (Image 25).

Naturally reared pups are raised to be as healthy as possible and come from generations of raw fed animals, therefore a Biologically Appropriate Raw Food diet is recommended (Billinghurst, 2001). It is important to allow the mother the ability to continue to feed the pups naturally if she wants to, as in the wild they would for several months (Mason, 1973).

Image 24 (Turner, 2008)

Image 25 (Turner, 2008)

Socialisation and exercise is vital (see Images 26 & 27) for the future mental health and trainability of each puppy (Fennell, 2005):

Image 26 (Turner, 2005)

Image 27 (Turner, 2007)

Individual personalities will begin to be evident from four weeks, and from 4-6 weeks a good indication of adherence to breed standard is evident.

At eight weeks, in line with Kennel Club rules and ethics, and the Animal Welfare Act (2006), puppies can go to their new homes.

Veterinary health checks are the trademark of responsible breeding, can be obtained in writing from you local veterinary surgeon and can be given in the puppy pack as re-assurance of quality (see Appendix 3 for example). Homoeopathic vaccines, called nosodes can be given from 10 weeks of age, are proposed to be a healthier alternative than chemical vaccines (Day, 2007), and last the lifetime of the animals (see Appendix 4 for example of vaccine record performed by a homoeopathic veterinary surgeon, please note that this card states that regular vaccines are 'essential', however current advice from the World Small Animal

Veterinary Association states that annual vaccines are inadvisable and in fact un-necessary, (WSAVA, 2010)).

Responsible home placing

Much care must be taken by the breeder to recognise the difference between pet and breed quality puppies and the potential home that each goes to. Breeding restrictions can be placed on the pups Kennel Club registration by the breeder, and can at a later date be lifted by the breeder, but not by the owner.

Each pup should be re-homed with a Puppy Pack containing:

- Registration Certificate
- Pedigree
- Advice sheet, including advice on
  - Feeding
  - Worming
  - Vaccination/Natural Immunity
  - Exercise
  - & how to get in touch with any questions (see Appendix 5)
- Insurance (6 weeks puppy insurance is available via PetPlan, however will not cover for 'vaccine preventable diseases' if the animal is not vaccinated)

Ensure that any potential owner is as in love with their puppy as the pup is with them (Image 28) and that they know should anything adverse occur, they can always get in touch for advice and/or return the pup for any reason. This provides security for the new owner, and for the pup, as whilst you may choose the potential home very carefully, life changes occur in which you may need to take the pup back at a later stage, better this than they end up in rescue or worse.

Image 28 (Turner, 2005)

Some breeders require more than simply a phone interview, and observation of the potential owners with the puppies, and have their own questionnaire which they compete for their own personal records when doing a home check.

An example of a home check questionnaire:-

Name of Applicant
Address
Post Code
Telephone Numbers, home & mobile
Area: Town or Rural
Type of Property
Is the property owned or rented
Proof of identity: photo identity preferred showing name and address
Number of adults and/or children living in the property
Ages of children
Are children familiar with dogs
Are visiting children familiar with dogs
How many hours on average would the dog be home alone
Where would the dog be whilst home alone
How big is the garden
Paved or grass
Is the garden secure
How high is the fencing
Are there any objects that could be used as a platform to escape
Are there any dangers i.e. pond
Is there side or rear access and if so is it secure
Is the property near to a main road
Are there any animals already in residence
Breed & age of resident dogs
Sex and neutered status
Feeding & health regime
Temperament

How would introduction be handled
Are there any visiting animals
How would introduction to visiting animals be handled
Are there any other pets in the home? Detail
How would you separate pets if necessary
Is anyone in the home banned from keeping pets
Details of experience of dog ownership
Who would exercise the dog and how often
Would the dog have full run of the house
If not, which rooms would be out of bounds
Where would the dog sleep
Would the dog need to travel in a car, if so where would they be going and how far away is that
How would the dog be secured in the car
What would be the arrangements for the dog if/when the applicant went on holiday
Would the temporary accommodation accept the feeding and health regime
Are there any plans to relocate in the next 12 months
If you relocated and were unable to take the dog with you, what would you do with him/her
Have the financial implications of ownership been considered
Do you intend to take out pet insurance, and if not what are the contingency plans in an emergency

How would you deal with:
    Chewing
    Messing in the house
    Barking/howling
    Nipping
    Aggression towards dogs
    Aggression towards people

Food/Toy aggression Lead pulling Separation anxiety Destructive behaviour Long term health problems
Do you have a local vet
Do you have transport if necessary to the veterinary surgery

In Conclusion

Meticulous planning of many generations of dogs, whilst taking into account health, temperament and adherence to the breed standard is the only responsible way forward for the future of naturally reared pets, and must be co-ordinated carefully between breeders and the breed club.

If you think that you can improve the breed with your litter, then by all means go ahead. Be prepared for a distinct lack of sleep, and constant cleaning, as well as the necessity to turn away many potential homes because you do not consider them good enough.

Understand that you will fall in love with all of the pups, some more than others, and that to let them go will be both a huge heart ache and a relief. The rewards of raising a litter are not financial, they are emotional, whilst it is a roller-coaster (especially when morning the loss of treasured items smashed in play), when puppies, with no ulterior motive, choose to come up to you and play with your, or even fall asleep on you, your heart will melt.

Also, be prepared, that if you cannot find the right homes, you may need to keep a number of pups, or even the entire litter, long term or permanently.

Appendix 1

The Kennel Club General Code of Ethics

All breeders who register their puppies, and new owners who register ownership of their dogs with the Kennel Club, accept the jurisdiction of the Kennel Club and undertake to abide by its general Code of Ethics.

Breeders/Owners:

1. Will properly house, feed, water and exercise all dogs under their care and arrange for appropriate veterinary attention if and when required.
2. Will agree without reservation that any veterinary surgeon who performs an operation on any of their dogs which alters the natural conformation of the animal, or who carries out a caesarean section on a bitch, may report such operations to the Kennel Club.
3. Will agree that no healthy puppy will be culled. Puppies which may not conform to the Breed Standard should be placed in suitable homes.
4. Will abide by all aspects of the Animal Welfare Act.
5. Will not create demand for, nor supply, puppies that have been docked illegally.
6. Will agree not to breed from a dog or bitch which could be in any way harmful to the dog or to the breed.
7. Will not allow any of their dogs to roam at large or to cause a nuisance to neighbours or those carrying out official duties.
8. Will ensure that their dogs wear properly tagged collars and will be kept leashed or under effective control when away from home.
9. Will clean up after their dogs in public places or anywhere their dogs are being exhibited.
10. Will only sell dogs where there is a reasonable expectation of a happy and healthy life and will help with the re-homing of a dog if the initial circumstances change.
11. Will supply written details of all dietary requirements and give guidance concerning responsible ownership when placing dogs in a new home.
12. Will ensure that all relevant Kennel Club documents are provided to the new owner when selling or transferring a dog, and will

agree, in writing, to forward any relevant documents at the earliest opportunity, if not immediately available.

13. Will not sell any dog to commercial dog wholesalers, retail pet dealers or directly or indirectly allow dogs to be given as a prize or donation in a competition of any kind. Will not sell by sale or auction Kennel Club registration certificates as stand alone items (not accompanying a dog).

14. Will not knowingly misrepresent the characteristics of the breed nor falsely advertise dogs nor mislead any person regarding the health or quality of a dog.

Breach of these provisions may result in expulsion from club membership, and/or disciplinary action by the Kennel Club and/or reporting to the relevant authorities for legal action, as appropriate.

Last updated - January 2011

(Kennel Club, 2011)

Appendix 2

Accredited Breeder Scheme Requirements and Recommendations

The Scheme currently has the following **requirements**

Accredited Breeders must:

Ensure that all breeding stock is Kennel Club registered.

Hand over the dog's registration certificate at time of sale if available, or forward it to the new owner as soon as possible. Explain any endorsements that might pertain and obtain written and signed confirmation from the new owner, at or before the date on which the dog is physically transferred, that the new owner is aware of the endorsement(s), regardless of whether or not the endorsed registration certificate is available.

- Follow Kennel Club policy regarding maximum age and number/frequency of litters
- Permanently identify breeding stock by DNA profile, microchip, or tattoo
- Make use of health screening schemes, relevant to their breed, on all breeding stock. These schemes include DNA testing, hip dysplasia, elbow dysplasia and inherited eye conditions
- Socialise the puppies and provide written advice, in the Puppy Sales Wallet, on continuation of socialisation, exercise and future training
- Provide written advice, in the scheme Puppy Sales Wallet, on feeding and worming programmes
- Provide a written record, in the Puppy Sales Wallet, on the immunisation measures taken
- Provide reasonable post-sales telephone advice
- Inform buyers of the requirements and the recommendations that apply to Kennel Club Accredited Breeders as well as the existence of the complaints procedure

- Draw up a contract of sale (see below link) for each puppy and provide a copy in the Puppy Sales Wallet.
- Provide a list of breed specific traits and tendencies or any further breed specific advice or information that may enhance the puppy buyers understanding of the breed they are buying.

Kennel Club Accredited Breeder Guide to content of a sales contract

In addition there are a number of **recommendations**

Accredited Breeders are strongly encouraged to:

- Make sure that whelping facilities accord with good practice
- The contract of sale should clearly lay out to the buyer the nature and details of any guarantee given (e.g. time limit) and/or any provisions for refund or return and replacement of puppy. If endorsements are being used the contract should also explain why these have been placed and under what circumstances they would be removed (if any). The contract should be signed and dated by both breeder and purchaser, showing that both have agreed to these terms
- Commit to help, if necessary, with the re-homing of a dog, for whatever reason, throughout the dog's lifetime
- Follow relevant breed health screening recommendations.

(Kennel Club, 2008)

Appendix 3

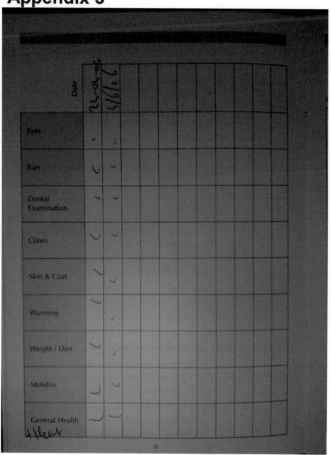

Date	24-05-06	21/9/9										
Eyes	✓	✓										
Ears	✓	✓										
Dental Examination	✓	✓										
Claws	✓	✓										
Skin & Coat	✓	✓										
Worming	✓	✓										
Weight / Diet	✓	✓										
Mobility	✓	✓										
General Health	✓	✓										

(Turner, 2005)

71

Appendix 4

(Turner, 2005)

Appendix 5

Your puppy has been carefully bred for type and temperament, with every effort to produce the very best of what is a beautiful breed.

Your puppy has been wormed at 2, 4, 6 & 8 weeks, and will need repeat treatment at 12 weeks, and then again every three months until one year of age.

Vaccinations:

Your puppy has been homoeopathically vaccinated by a homeopathic veterinary surgeon, the certificate from which is in this pack. Your pup will never need another vaccination, if you are worried about kennelling whilst away, I will be happy to take him/her for the duration of your vacation, or can recommend kennels who accept homoeopathic remedies.

Your puppy is fed on a species appropriate diet:

- 8 parts raw meaty bones,
- 2 parts crushed fruit and vegetables
- 2 parts offal,
- 1 part supplements

The amount is dependent on how much your puppy will eat, always give too much rather than not enough. Your puppy should be nice and plump but not over fat. Increase the amount fed as the puppy grows.

A bowl of fresh water must be available at all times.

Should you have any questions on feeding over and above the information given to you whilst being interviewed about potential ownership, please feel free to come back to me at any time.

I strongly recommend just light exercise, for the first 4-5 weeks with NO road pounding. Free running is by far the best for young growing bones, but light exercise on a hard surface will help keep your puppy's nails short and his/her feet tight. Increase the duration and distance of exercise slowly as your puppy grows. Remember when out with your puppy always take a poop scoop/nappy sacks with you and clean up their deposits.

If you have to part with your dog/bitch for any reason in the future, you MUST first contact me, as you know how carefully I place my precious babies, and fear not knowing where, and how they are, and I will assist you in re-homing or re-home him/her myself.

If you have any queries or concerns please do not hesitate to get in touch, (a photo and update would be much appreciated from time to time).

Most of all I wish you every happiness with your puppy.

Breeder Name

Breeder Address

Breeder Phone Numbers

Breeder Email Address

Breeder web address

References

AMP (2010) *Whelping & Kittening Boxes.* (Internet) Available from:
http://www.whelping-boxes.co.uk (accessed 05/03/2011)

BBC (2009) *Firm Hails Dog Clone Breakthrough.* (Internet) Available from:
http://news.bbc.co.uk/1/hi/world/asia-pacific/7858566.stm (accessed
06/03/2011)

Billinghurst, I. (2001) *The Barf Diet.* Warrigal Publishing, New South Wales

Carricato. A.M. (1992) *Veterinary Notes for Dog Breeders.* MacMillan
Publishing Company, New York p. 3-30, 88-92, 95-156

Crown (2006) *Animal Welfare Act 2006.* (Internet) Available from:
http://www.legislation.gov.uk/ukpga/2006/45/contents (accessed 06/03/2011)

Day, C. (2007) *Nosode Protection.* Alternative Veterinary Medicine Centre.
WS023/07, Oxford

Eldredge, D.M. Carlson, Carlson, L.D. Carlson, D.G. & Giffin, J.M.(2007) *Dog
Owner's Home Veterinary Handbook.* Howell Book House. New Jersey p. 57

Evans, J.M. & White, K. (1988) *The Book of the Bitch.* Henstons Ltd, High
Wycombe p. 50-51

Fennel, J. (2005) *The Seven Ages of your Dog.* Harper Collins, London p. 22-
63

Frankling, E. (1987) *Practical Dog Breeding and Genetics.* Popular Dogs,
London p. 166-183

Gough, A. & Thomas, A. (2004) *Breed Predispositions to Disease in Dogs
and Cats.* Blackwell Publishing, Oxford p. 13-14, 72-79, 145-146

Holst, P.A. (2000) *Canine Reproduction.* Alpine Publications, Loveland p. 45,
65-66, 98-101, 163-176

Kennel Club (2006) *BVA/KC Health Schemes.* (Internet) Available from:
http://www.thekennelclub.org.uk/item/308 (accessed 05/03/2011)

Kennel Club, 2 (2006) *DNA Profiling.* (Internet) Available from:
http://www.thekennelclub.org.uk/item/463/ (accessed 05/03/2011)

Kennel Club, 3 (2006) *Artificial Insemination (AI).* (Internet) Available from:
http://www.thekennelclub.org.uk/item/478 (accessed 06/03/2011)

Kennel Club (2008) *Accredited Breeder Scheme Requirements and Recommendations.* (Internet) Available from: http://www.thekennelclub.org.uk/item/2158 (accessed 05/03/2011)

Kennel Club (2010) *Information Guide – DNA Profiling and Parentage Analysis.* (Internet) Available from: http://www.thekennelclub.org.uk/item/1077 (accessed 01/04/2011)

Kennel Club (2011) *The Kennel Club General Code of Ethics.* (Internet) Available from: http://www.thekennelclub.org.uk/item/247 (accessed 05/03/2011)

Lane, D.R. & Cooper, B. (2003) *BSAVA Veterinary Nursing.* Elsevier, Philidelphia p. 392

Lee, B.C. Kim, M.K. Jang, G. Oh, H.J. Yuda, F, Kim, H. J. Samin, M.H. Kim, J.J. Kang, S.K. Schatten, G. & Hwang, W.S. (2005) Dogs Cloned from Adult Somatic Cells. *Nature.* 436, 641 (4 August 2005)

Loi, P. Beaujean, N. Khochbin, S. Fulka, J. & Ptak, G. (2008) Asymmetric Nuclear Reprogramming in Somatic Cell Nuclear Transfer? *BioEssays* Vol 30 Issue 1, January 2008 p. 66-74

Mason, B. (1973) *Cry of the Wild.* (Film Documentary) National Film Board of Canada. Montreal

McLeavy, A. (1996) *Pet Owner's Guide to The Border Collie.* Ringpress, Gloucester p. 66

Mech, L.D. (1970) *The Wolf.* University of Minnesota Press, Minneapolis p. 113-114

Neville, P. (1993) *Pet Sex – The Rude Facts of Life for the Family Dog, Cat and Rabbit.* Sidgwick and Jackson, London p. 62

Ogonuki, N. Inoue, K. Yamamoto, Y. Noguchi, Y. Tanemura, K. Suzuki, O. Nakayama, H. Doi, K. Ohtomo, Y. Satoh, M. Nishida, A. & Ogura, A. (2002) Early Death of Mice Cloned from Somatic Cells. *Nature Genetics.* 30, (1 March 2002) p253-254

Olson, C.D. (2009) Does Prenatal Ultrasound Increase Risk of Autism? *The Journal of the American Osteopathic Association.* 109[2]:71-72

Penn, D.J. (2002) The Scent of Genetic Compatibility: Sexual Selection and the Major Histocompatibility Complex. *Ethology.* 108[1]:1-21

Petlife (2011) *Vetbed Original.* (Internet) Available from:
http://www.petlifeonline.co.uk/Store/Dogs/Bedding/Vetbed-Original (accessed 05/03/2011)

Petlife (2011) *Welpi – Milk for Dogs.* (Internet) Available from:
http://www.petlifeonline.co.uk/Store/Dogs/Care/Welpi-$9-Milk-for-Dogs
(accessed 01/04/2011)

Pottenger, F. (1983) *Pottenger's Cats – A Study in Nutrition*, Price-Pottenger Foundation Inc, California

Riviere, J.E. & Papich, M.G. (2009) *Veterinary Pharmacology and Therapeutics.* Wiley Blackwell, Iowa p. 724

Robinson, S. (2005) Photographs copyright of Serena Robinson

Root Kustriitz, M.V. (2006) *The Dog Breeder's Guide to Successful Breading and Health Management.* Elsevier Inc. St. Louis p. 159-160

Thomassen, R. Farstad, W. Krogenaes, A. Fougner, J.A. & Berg, K.A. (2001) Artificial Insemination with Frozen Semen in Dogs: A Retrospective Study. *Journal of Reproduction and Fertility Supplement*, 57 p. 341-346

Turner, H.B. (2004) Photographs copyright of Hope Turner

Turner, H.B. (2005) Photographs copyright of Hope Turner

Turner, H.B. (2007) Photographs copyright of Hope Turner

Turner, H.B. (2008) Photographs copyright of Hope Turner

Turner, H.B. (2013) Photographs copyright of Hope Turner

Turner, H B (2013) *The Science Behind Canine Raw Feeding.* Talen Publications, UK

Williams, E.L. & Casanova, M.F. (2011) Above Genetics: Lessons from Cerebral Development in Autism. *Translational Neuroscience.* 2[2]:106-220

Williams, J. (2009) *The Complete Textbook of Animal Health and Welfare.* Elsevier, Edinburgh p. 165-171

WSAVA (2010) *Vaccination Guidelines* [Internet] Available from:
http://www.wsava.org/guidelines/vaccination-guidelines (Accessed 04/11/2013)

Useful Links:

American Holistic Veterinary Medical Association	www.ahvma.org
Association of Non-Veterinary Natural Animal Health Pracitioners	www.annahp.co.uk
British Association of Homoeopathic Veterinary Surgeons	www.bahvs.com
Canine Health Concern	www.canine-health-concern.org.uk
Chip Me Not	www.chipmenot.com
Healthful	www.healthful.uk.com
I'm A Puppy Mummy	www.ImAPuppyMummy.com
Neem Genie	www.neemgenie.co.uk
Price Pottenger Nutrition Foundation	www.ppnf.org
Raw Food Vets	www.rawfoodvets.com
Verm-X	www.verm-x.com

Recommended Reading

Allport, R. (2001) *Natural Healthcare for Pets.* Element Books Ltd. London, UK

Allport, R. (2010) *Healing Your Dog the Natural Way.* Remember When. Yorkshire, UK.

Billinghurst, I. (2001) *The BARF Diet.* Warrigal Publishing. New South Wales, Australia

Day, C. (1998) *The Homoeopathic Treatment of Small Animals.* Rider Books. London, UK

De Baïracli Levy (1992) *The Complete Herbal Handbook for the Dog and Cat.* Faber and Faber. London, UK

Fisher, S. (2007) *Unlock Your Dogs Potential.* David & Charles Ltd. Ohio, USA

Martin, A. (2003) *Food Pets Die For.* Newsage Press. Oregon, USA

O'Driscoll, C. (2005) *Shock To The System.* Abbeywood Publishing. Angus, Scotland

Pottenger, F.M. (1995) *Pottenger's Cats.* Price-Pottenger Nutrition Foundation. California, USA

Rugaas, T. (2006) *On Talking Terms With Dogs: Calming Signal.* Dogwise Publishing. Washington, USA

Turner, H.B. (2013) *The Science Behind Canine Raw Feeding.* Talen Publications. Cambridge, UK

Withers, A.K.L. (2013) *Wish Come True.* Wishie Publications. Edinburgh, UK

Printed in Great Britain
by Amazon.co.uk, Ltd.,
Marston Gate.